The No-Nonsense Guide to Blizzard Safety

Jeffery D. Sims

Books may be purchased by contacting the publisher and author at Lulu.com, Amazon.com, or contact the author at:

Beyond The Spectrum Books
http://beyond-the-political-spectrum.blogspot.com/

Cover Design: Jeffery D. Sims
Publisher: Lulu Books & Beyond The Spectrum Books
ISBN: ISBN 978-1-304-70939-4
1. Reference 2. Science 3. Weather 4. Safety 5. Blizzards
First Edition
Printed in North Carolina, USA

Acknowledgement

The following is a list of the people I'd like to thank for believing in me and my dreams:

... (no, I didn't skip anyone).

Table of Contents

Introduction

Simply put, in some ways I was a normal child while in other ways, I was anything but. It is the abnormal part of my being which accounts for why you are holding this book in your hot little hands (or reading it on your tablet). While I enjoyed watching cartoons, reading comic books, and favored science-fiction (notice a pattern?), I was also fascinated—infatuated actually—with learning about strange, unusual, and otherwise unexplained uncommon events. Whether the subject was verifying the legitimacy of alleged occurrences explored in the field of parapsychology, learning about what things exist beyond the boundaries of our planet through the area of astronomy, or—of relevance to you the reader—understanding the causes of interesting weather phenomenon like tornadoes and hurricanes.

As an adult, my love of learning had grown to encompass many other subjects, including history and politics (which I went to college to study). I had come to the awareness that I had/have an innate thirst for knowledge, about everything around me. As a result, I have more books than I will ever read, probably more than the average person. I've also probably had more different types of jobs than the average person. I've done a great deal of living. And in everything I've read, done, and observed, I've taken a great deal of awareness about life and the nature of the universe around us with me (yes, I know...a little grandiose, if not self-centered-sounding). I suppose by way of osmosis, I had also developed a love of teaching after having fallen into the vocation of substitute and adult education instructor. Because of these experiences, I have been driven to observe the world with an attempt to gain a deeper meaning of it all...and maybe bring a little bit of insight to others.

I am also driven to write about my observations –without the latent bias of emotion, beliefs, or cultural beliefs—in order to convey a semblance of truth (the "teacher" in me I suppose) and maybe give others a little something to think about. This is why I started blogging and writing regularly some years ago. In an indirect way, writing is also a way for me to help others to think about and offer possible solutions to grander problems posed by counterproductive policies and our own individual thinking. But it was only recently that I was motivated to combine my proclivity for (objective) observation, thirst for learning, and ultimately my writing to create a series of books based on my own intellectual curiosities and love for seeking solutions to existing problems.

This resulting compendium of interests and ideas has the (intended) benefit of imparting in those who chose to purchase and read it a level of awareness and knowledge about the an aspect of the dangers –those presented by the earth we live on—inherent in the world around us. And although there are no certain safe places to hide from real-life dangers, there *are* places as well as courses of actions that one can take to limit exposure to these dangers. I acknowledge this fact throughout the book(s) by using terms like *relatively*, *comparatively*, or variations of such words to convey that the suggestions offered are in, all likelihood based on research and other findings, the best options given the dangers and circumstances.

It is my hope that the information in this book (or as I call it, "safety manual") will save a life, or at least prevent serious injury to those who would might be affected by a related dangerous experience.

So without further ado, I present to you, the No-Nonsense Guide to Blizzard Safety...
--Jeffery D. Sims

Blizzards

What Are They?

The term "blizzard" is the applied description of a particular type of severe winter weather snowstorm. A blizzard is characterized by the presence of strong sustained winds of 35 mph (56 km/h) or higher, cold temperatures, and visibility reduced by falling and/or blowing snow to less than 1/4th of a mile (less than 400 m). Additionally, the criteria of high winds and reduced visibility must be sustained for 3 consecutive hours for a snowstorm to be considered an official blizzard. However, these are but the minimum-level criteria for what constitutes one of these severe winter storms; in most blizzards, the individual conditions tend to far exceed the set minimal. The winds of most blizzards routinely howl *in excess* of the 35mph (56 km/h) threshold, while low visibility due to falling and blowing snow is usually of a longer duration than 3 hours. The temperatures during a blizzard can fall well below 0 degrees Fahrenheit (-17 Celsius). This is especially true in blizzard-prone regions around the world.

Blizzards, especially severe blizzards can and often *do* create life-threatening conditions. For example, traveling by automobile in these storms can become difficult (or even impossible) due to reduced or near-zero visibility and rapidly accumulating snow amounts—setting up the perfect conditions for calamities on the roads. Also, the strong winds and cold temperatures accompanying blizzards can combine to create dangerously unhealthy *wind chills* (the lowering of air temperatures caused by blowing wind as it affects the rate of heat-loss from the human body from exposed skin). What's more, people have died attempting to remove the heavy amounts of snow after a blizzard has passed. Finally, the conditions involving a blizzard can hinder or even prevent emergency and rescue personnel from helping those who may need life-or-death assistance during one of these extreme snowstorms, resulting in possible prolonged injuries and/or death. This is because blizzards tend to brings most normal activity in areas where they occur to a standstill due to the impeding of traffic and other related travel. Under these circumstances, blizzards can impact a region's short-term economic stability by restricting or even halting day-to-day commerce-related activities. In worst-case scenarios,

The aftermath of a 2011 blizzard in Chicago, Illinois. The city of Chicago is well-known for harsh winter weather and the occasional blizzard.

blizzards can cause property damage and inflict widespread casualties—especially in underdeveloped regions of the world where they might occur.

Above: The damage left in the wake of a Blizzard in the city of Boston, Massachusetts (Courtesy of CBS television, Boston). Below: The aftermath of the 2008 Afghanistan Blizzard, among the deadliest on record (aliraqi.org).

How Do They Form?

   Like many other examples of extreme weather, blizzards require a particular set of atmospheric conditions as well as specific weather "ingredients" to come together in order to form. The conditions involving the formation of blizzards tend to congregate within the influence of the *jet stream*, the river of strong air currents that flow high in the atmosphere that influence the Earth's climatic patterns.[1]

   Generally, a blizzard starts high in the clouds with tiny super-cooled water droplets (these water droplets can remain in this extreme cold state of all the way down to -40 Fahrenheit/-40 Celsius). While aloft, many of these droplets encounter particles of dust, also found in the air. As this happens, the super-cooled water droplets will freeze around these dust partials, forming ice crystals. At this point, random water vapor molecules begin to attach, collect, and grow as small lumps on each ice crystal. We recognize these "lumps" as the familiar and individually-unique geometric shapes of a snowflake, which forms around each dust particle.

   Specifically, the atmospheric conditions needed for blizzards to form tend to do so around three individual elements, which need to be present for a blizzard to become active. The first of these is *cold air*. Freezing temperatures must be present both at ground level as well as in the clouds where snowflakes form. If warmer temperatures were present, particularly at ground level will cause any snow formed in the clouds to melt while falling to earth, resulting instead in either rain or *freezing rain* (liquid precipitation that forms and falls as raindrops that immediately freezes as it hits cold surfaces at ground-level). The second (and somewhat obvious) ingredient needed for blizzards to form is cloud-based moisture that eventually becomes precipitation. Moisture present in the air eventually combines with the proper temperature[2] to form and provide the necessary water vapor that eventually becomes the signature heavy falling and blowing snow of blizzards. The final component needed for the creation of a blizzard is—oddly enough—rising warmer air needed to create clouds and cause precipitation. This warm air must rise over the colder air, which may happen in 1 of 2 ways. The first way is for existing winds (such as jet streams) to pull colder polar air down toward warmer regions such as those found near closer to the equator, while bringing warmer air toward the poles from these warmer regions. The second way is when warmer air is sent aloft of colder air at higher elevations. As the warmer air rises, it forms clouds as it flows up a mountainside; the result is a rapidly forming mountaintop blizzard. For non-mountaintop blizzards, these ingredients will combine with a series of necessary conditions to create the setup for a blizzard.

   For blizzards to develop, these [required] individual and general components become active within specific weather patterns that organize in colder weather. Blizzards tend to occur when the jet stream(s) in the upper atmosphere "sags" to the south, pulling polar air found in northern colder regions into warmer humid air to the south. The result is a clash of opposing air masses that often create high winds, not unlike those found at similarly intersecting air masses where spring thunderstorms form. Along this region of atmospheric instability, the presence of the increased moisture in the air, high winds, and the appropriate temperatures—the aforementioned ingredients—start the dynamics of a

---

[1] Jet streams affect weather patterns around the world by pushing large masses of air that forming weather systems "ride" toward other systems, which in extreme cases can cause violent weather outbreaks.

[2] The "proper temperatures" are crucial for the formation of the heavy snow component of a blizzard, as very cold air does not make very much snow.

potential blizzard. When all of these conditions are present, the result is the driving winds and heavy and blowing snow we identify with blizzards.

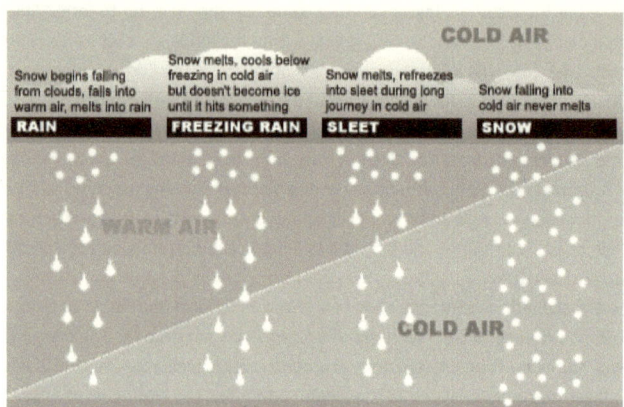

An illustration of how warm and cold air interacts to form various forms of precipitation. The final stage of this diagram indicates the formation of a blizzard's chief ingredient, snow.

And like all other weather occurrences, no two blizzards are alike. For example, snow storms—particularly blizzards—tend to produce a different brand of snow. Some snow is of the fluffy, "powdery" type. Powdery snow is composed of mostly. In fact, snowflakes making up this type of snow are made up of 95% air. And despite how much of this type of snow falls and blows during a blizzard, most snowflakes of this type never make it to the ground. But because this type of snow is lighter, it is easily blown around by high winds more readily, affecting visibility and creating dangerous conditions for those who find themselves outside during a blizzard. However, if a snowflake falls through a cloud with lower temperatures and humidity, thousands of super-cooled droplets will attach to its surface. This increased level of moisture within this type of snow makes it heavier. This type of heavy "wet" snow accumulates at a greater rate than the lighter, fluffy type. The result is usually higher snow totals with its own set of dangers.

Although the specific weather-related criteria that constitute an actual blizzard (the high winds and extremely low visibility criteria being met for at least 3 consecutive hours) may be present, every heavy snowstorm is *not* a blizzard—even when snow accumulations are excessive. For example, heavy *lake-effect snowstorms*[3] are not blizzards, even in the presence of comparatively heavy winds. Likewise, *snow squalls* (small pockets of sudden heavy snow that are usually accompanied by gusty winds close to

[3] Lake-effect snowstorms are a cold-weather, winter-related weather phenomenon that occurs when cold moves over large bodies of warmer waters of large lakes. As the warm lake water warms and/or heats layer of air closest to the surface, lake moisture evaporates into the cold air. The lighter and less dense warmer air begins to rise and cool. The moisture that evaporates into the air condenses and forms clouds, and snow begins to fall. If there is a continuous influx of this colder air over warmer waters, heavy lake-effect snow is the result. Whereas true blizzards tend to occur over a large area, lake-effect snowstorms form within narrow bands f snow-producing clouds. The rates of snowfall during particularly heavy lake-effect snow events may exceed 5 inches (over 12 centimeters) an hour, for several hours within this narrow corridor of inclimate weather. This means 10 to 15 miles (16 to 24 kilometers) on either side of that narrow band of heavy snow, skies may actually be sunny...with no snow at all.

ground surface) create *whiteout*[4] conditions similar to those seen in blizzards, but are more geographically localized events of a briefer duration. On the other hand, falling snow isn't always present to in a blizzard. In some cases, several inches/centimeters of snow on the ground can be whipped up by and blown around by strong winter winds. These winds can blow and whip up snow covering the ground enough to the point where visibility is similarly limited (or not possible) as one would find in an actual blizzard. This is what's known as a *ground blizzard*.

During ground blizzards, blizzard conditions may be present in only a portion of a general area experiencing a snowstorm. Ground blizzards will oftentimes occur in either sparsely populated or low-density populated areas where there is less development and therefore fewer obstructions such as tall buildings to block winds. An example of this are the open (i.e., rural) areas usually found outside of cities in the Midwestern regions of the U.S. and Central Canada during the height of winter. In more densely-populated urban areas, ground blizzards are highly uncommon due to the difficulty high winds are arable to blow snow around unfettered by physical obstructions. By comparison, blizzards are true storms, forming from an actual weather system in the same way that spring storms form.

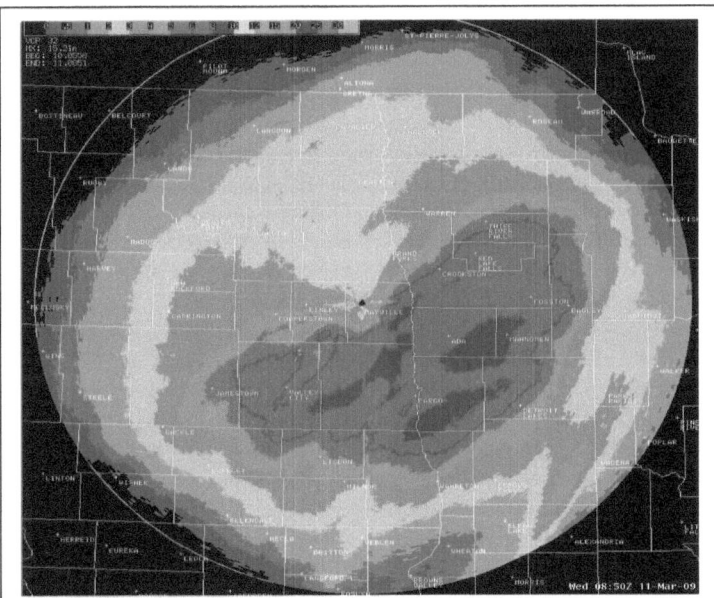

Radar image of the blizzard which occurred in an area of North Dakota on March 9-10, 2009. The darker colors indicate the heaviest snowfall over the 14-hour period the blizzard raged over the area—an estimated 6 -10 inches (15.24 – 25.4 centimeters).

What Makes Them Dangerous?

---

[4] *Whiteouts* are one of the many dangerous conditions created by blizzards, especially as they relate to travelling. This phenomenon will be discussed in more detail under the next section, *What Makes Them Dangerous*.

Blizzards are one of the few natural occurrences whereby each of their singular elements—the extreme cold, high winds, and blinding snow—pose individual as well as collective dangers for those who might be impacted by them. As one might expect, the wind-enhanced cold temperatures is often the most immediate threat posed by blizzards.

Individuals who might suddenly find themselves travelling through a blizzard, or outdoors when one begins are at serious risk for cold-related issues that are potentially life-threatening. One of these dangers is *hypothermia*. Hypothermia is a medical condition that results when the human body is exposed to extremely cold temperatures for an extended period of time. The condition onsets when the body experiences a loss of heat at a rate faster than the body can be generate it, causing a dangerously low body temperature (normal body temperature is around 98.6 F/37 C). Hypothermia is said to occur when the body's temperature passes below the 95 F (35 C) threshold. When the body's temperature drops, the body's organs and nervous system no longer function properly. Blood begins to cool during this process, and is transported through the body's circulation system to all other parts of the body. This includes the extremities. It is partially for this reason that the areas that are farthest away from the main part of our bodies—fingers and toes—tend to become cold the fastest. Cooled blood flowing to the brain often results in impaired cognitive thought- processing. And the longer an unprotected, unheated body is exposed to the cold, the faster hypothermic conditions are likely to set in. What's more, a person becomes even *more* susceptible to hypothermia if they are wearing clothes (especially in extreme weather conditions such as a blizzard) that become wet from exposure to moisture. Left untreated, hypothermia can eventually lead to more cold-related complications, including complete failure of the heart and respiratory system...eventually resulting in death.

Hypothermia was the primary cause of death for between 200 – 500 people—many of them school aged children—living in America's Great Plains region in January of 1888. On January 12th of that year, an unexpected blizzard sprang up on the heels of an unusually warm winter day. Although the weather patterns that contributed to the formation of this intense blizzard began gathering on the 11th, all the active elements of the blizzard came together over a period of a few hours on the 12th. Within a few hours, rapid temperature drops of between 20 and 40 degrees in the region began occurring, accompanied by high winds and heavy snow. What made this blizzard particularly deadly was the fact that blizzard conditions began to set into the region during the hours when most adults were at work, and children were in school. Because of the period of unusual warmth prior to the blizzard's arrival, many children went to school without the winter attire—gloves/mittens, booths, and heavy coats—usually worn during the time of year. As schools were dismissed during the day, many children were caught unawares outdoors during the height of the blizzard. Because so many children perished during this blizzard attempting to walk home from school, it has become known by most historical records as the "Schoolhouse Blizzard" and the "Children's Blizzard." Most of the deaths that occurred during this tragedy was the result of a combination of hypothermia brought on by exposure to the cold temperatures, the driving wet snow, and the fact that many attempting to find their way home simply could not see where they were headed...resulting in their becoming disoriented, lost, and thus prolonging their exposure to the elements.[5] About a quarter of the deaths associated with the winter

---

[5] The overwhelming number of deaths that came as a result of the "Schoolhouse Blizzard" of 1888 took place in the following states/territories:

season are due to individuals caught unawares outside during winter storm such as a blizzard. As in the case of the Schoolhouse Blizzard, most of those who begin experiencing the early stages of hypothermia fail to realize their imperiled health as their bodies get colder—until it is too late.

Another cold-related danger that blizzards can bring on is *frostbite*. Frostbite is the actual freezing of the body's skin that results when the blood flow through the body is reduced due to contracted blood vessels. This in turn causes a reduced level of oxygen to be circulated to the various parts of the body (oxygen normally supplied through this blood flow), causing a loss of sensation, and changes to affected tissue areas. Frostbite is usually brought on by prolonged exposure to cold temperatures, particularly if they are accompanied by low wind-chills such as those caused by blizzard conditions. As in the case of hypothermia, frostbite is most likely to affect parts of the body first that are farthest away from the body's center (and experience comparatively less blood flow on a regular basis). These include the feet, toes, hands, fingers, nose, and ears. Also like hypothermia, frostbite can go undetected by the victim during its initial onset. The only sign that anything may be amidst is the numbness in certain parts of the body that is often associated with being exposed to cold temperatures. However, as the body remains exposed, a level of severe frostbite can begin to set it, resulting in permanent damage to deep skin tissue (depending on how long and deeply the tissue was frozen). In the *most* severe cases of frostbite, blood flow to the affected area(s) may stop altogether, resulting in possible permanent damage to blood vessels, muscles, nerves, tendons...even the bones themselves. In extreme cases, the tissue will actually die due to irreversible damage at the cellular level. In these instances, the affected area(s) may need to be amputated.[6] Although more infrequent in the U.S. than in other parts of the world, frostbite in the states is not unheard of. Many of those who experience either hypothermia or frostbite do so either while travelling through an area experiencing harsh winter conditions, or as a result of long-term outdoor activities that may or may not be related to work or leisure activities.

Another of the more obvious dangers invariably posed by blizzards are the risks associated with the lack of visibility due to wind-driven and falling snow. Although walking in blizzard-reduced visibility has its own set of dangers (as illustrated by possibility of hypothermia and frostbite), most of the risks associated with the low visibility factor derive from attempting to drive and/or travel in such conditions. Whiteouts that occur over interstates and/or on major travel arteries can cause dangerous, potentially deadly traffic accidents as motorists' visibility might be reduced to near-zero levels. Approximately 70% of the total accidental deaths in the winter occur as a result of automobile accidents...caused in turn by hazardous weather and driving conditions.[7] In worst-case scenarios, multiple automobile traffic pile-ups can and do occur in these conditions. In 2010, a late December blizzard directly caused a 100-car interstate pileup near Fargo, North Dakota, stranding some would-be travelers after their automobiles were rendered inoperable after the massive car pileup. Fortunately, there were only a few minor injuries as a result of this incident. At other times, obscured visibility can have more tragic results. In 2006, a 22-vehicle pileup during another blizzard in Wyoming resulted in 6 deaths. Both cases illustrate

---

South Dakota (territory), North Dakota (territory), Montana (territory), Wyoming (territory), Idaho (territory), Nebraska, Minnesota. Numbers Compilations from the time are hard to pinpoint due to the loss of many public records (including death certificates), lost newspaper accounts, and because many bodies were not located for days or even months after the blizzard.

[6] Frostbite is a medical condition that varies in degrees of severity. For an explanation of these degrees, see Appendix C.

[7] For instructions and suggestions for how to drive in hazardous winter-related driving conditions, see Appendix D.

the fact that reduced visibility is exacerbated by the wide open spaces of a rural landscape. And while blizzards can and do affect urban as well as rural areas, the lack of visibility as a condition caused by these storms tends to be less serious in these more developed areas, where buildings and closely-built homes mitigate the effects of the increased winds and blinding snow.

The extreme cold temperatures produced in many blizzards can create hazards related to travel. Automobiles often stall in colder temperatures, especially if they haven't been properly maintained to endure the colder weather. Stalled automobiles cannot provide heat to keep warm. And being exposed to an absence of heat in an automobile during a blizzard can have obvious consequences (i.e., hypothermia). Additionally, the high winds and heavy wet snow can combine to snap electrical power lines, resulting in power outages that leave those without the ability to heat their homes subject to freezing temperatures...and the same potential issues as those exposed in an automobile under the same conditions. In February of 2011, a blizzard struck the city of Chicago, Illinois. During the height of this blizzard, hundreds of motorists became stranded on the city's famed Lake Shore Drive when snow accumulations and blinding wind made the major roadway artery impassible during the a high traffic period. A combination of stalled and blocked automobiles caused many motorists to abandon their cars, while others were trapped for many hours, opting not to challenge fate by venturing out in the harsh conditions.

Hundreds of abandoned vehicles were strewn along Chicago's Lake Shore Drive in the aftermath of the 2011 blizzard (Courtesy: Kiichiro Sato/Associated Press).

The snow itself can be yet another hazard inherent in blizzards. Depending upon their duration, severity, and amount of snowfall produced, blizzards can cause significant amounts of damage. Heavy snowfall, especially if the snow is of the heavy, moisture-packed type may accumulate up on the roofs of houses and other buildings. Though not a common occurrence, this accumulation of weight can cause roofs or entire buildings to collapse, especially buildings with flat roofs. In 2011, heavy snow caused the collapse of the roof of a senior center in Massachusetts after a heavy snow storm. The collapse trapped 2 people in the building, who were later freed. In addition, extreme blizzards have been known to down trees, snap power lines, and cause water and sewer pipes to rupture.

Another particular danger from blizzards lies more in the realms of the unseen and unsuspected. There is a great deal of preliminary evidence from years of research pointing to the increased incidence of heart attacks involving those attempting to remove show after a blizzard has passed. This link between blizzards, heavy snowfall, and shoveling is based on previous research studies published in many well-respected medical journals.[8] This conclusion behind this occurrence is based on the observation that snow-shoveling is creates increased demands on the body's cardiovascular system. This is because shoveling snow is an intense form exercise if you will, resulting in an increase of blood pressure. Furthermore, the cold temperatures that often linger in the aftermath of a heavy snowstorm/blizzard may be a contributing factor in that those forced to exert themselves physically attempting to remove snow tend to expend energy just to keep warm—which adds to the stress such activity places on the body. This is especially true if the type of snow is the type containing heavy amounts of moisture (i.e., "wet, heavy" snow"). And although the exact numbers are in dispute, there is little doubt that more than a few heart attacks occur throughout America annually due to exertion related to snow removal.[9]

Blizzards may not seem like a big deal on the face of it, but these severe winter storms can not only inconvenience day-to-day business activities, but can potentially cause property damage, create hazardous travelling conditions, and potential health concerns—all of which could result in serious injury or even death. All in all, blizzards affect about 26 million people on average annually, and result in an average of $572 million in damages due to property and business losses. The best way to avoid these potential hazards is to simply not underestimate the dangers posed by blizzards. Many of these potential dangers and how to best avoid them will be discussed later in the section entitled, "How To Prepare In The Event of a Blizzard?"

---

[8] Examples of established medical journals citing the link between shoveling snow in the aftermath of heavy snowstorms/blizzards and the increased incidence of heart attacks include:

"Snow shoveling: a trigger for acute myocardial infarction and sudden coronary death." American Journal of Cardiology 1996;77:855–858. and "Cardiac demands of heavy snow shoveling." JAMA (Journal of the American Medical Association). 1995;273:880–882.

[9] Depending on the study or source, the estimated number of deaths attributed to hear attacks range anywhere from 1,000 to 1,500 a year, with the overwhelming majority being males. However, other research that scrutinizes such figures indicates that, although this *is* in fact an yearly occurrence, the incidence of heart attacks due to shoveling snow may in fact be rare.

Damage from a blizzard occurring in and around Boston, Massachusetts in January, 2012.

The No-Nonsense Guide To Blizzard Safety

Where Do Blizzards Occur?

   Strictly speaking, any place on earth that is subject to normal seasonal changes that involve yearly winter conditions are at least vulnerable to the occasional blizzard. This means that blizzards are possible almost any place on earth, except for those regions nearest the equator where climatic patterns are limited to rainy and dry seasons. The presence of regular patterns that include winter conditions imply that weather extremes can take place within such seasonal norms. This means that at one end of the spectrum, unusually warm winters without blizzards can occur. At the other extreme point, unusually harsh winters can occur within these shifting climate regions—the point where and when blizzards can form. Among the many areas that are widely known to be common to blizzards is Europe, where strong blizzards form occasionally. Also, parts of Asia are susceptible to both weak and strong blizzards, especially the northern mountainous regions of the continent. But blizzards are most common in parts of Russia (especially Siberia) and surrounding countries, as well as northern and central parts of Canada. In the U.S., blizzards are most common in the northern Mississippi Basin, the Central Great Plains, regions surrounding the Great Lakes, and the Northeastern/New England region. In ad-

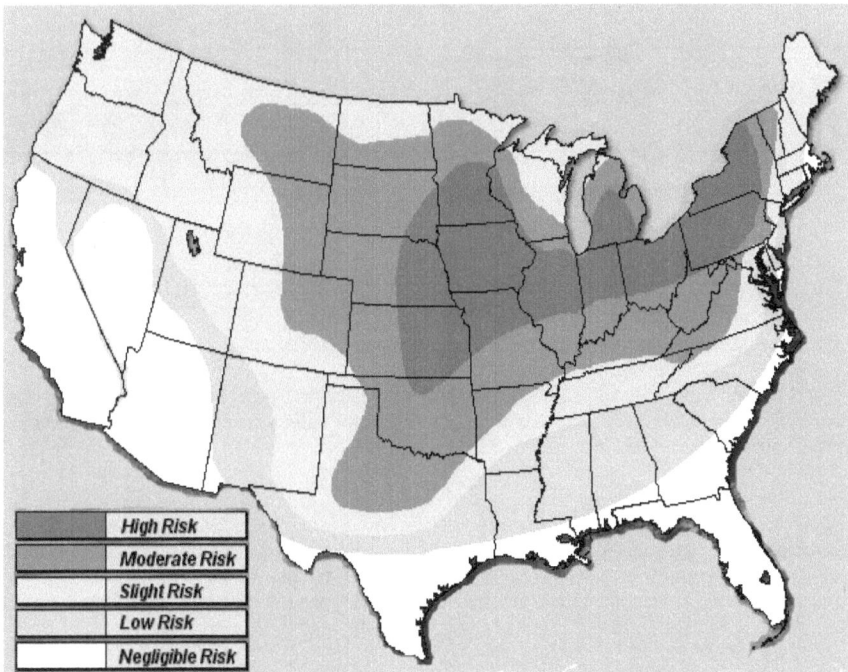

A map indicating the areas of the U.S. mainland susceptible to blizzards, based on yearly averages. The darker colors indicate the approximate highest occurrences of blizzards, with corresponding lighters colors indicating lesser chances (note: none of the shades regions indicate an absolute zero chance). Many of the highest risk/occurrences regions for blizzards correspond to the lake-effect "snow-belts" (see: next page).

dition, mountain blizzards are common on mountain peaks such as those around Mount Washington in New Hampshire and Mounts Rainier and McKinley in Washington and Alaska respectively.

The worst blizzards in the U.S. occur in the upper Plains. According to one study by Ball State University Professor Robert Schwartz, between 1959 through 2000, the states of North Dakota, South Dakota and Minnesota led the nation in the occurrence of severe (as well as the most) blizzards. [10]

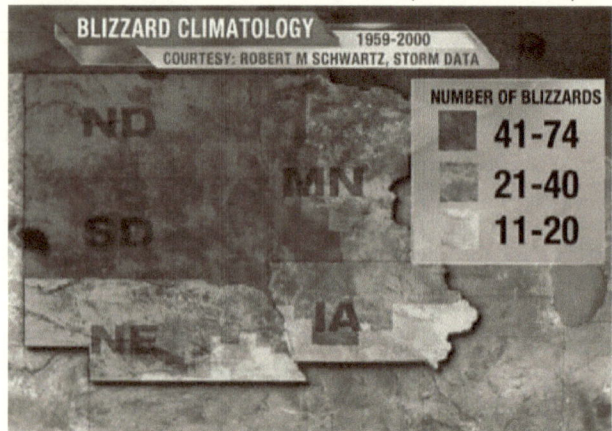

According to the study within this corridor of high blizzard activity, North and South Dakota in addition to areas of western Minnesota have the highest occurrence of blizzards every year. More specifically, the study also noted that:

- The most U.S. blizzards in a season is 27 in 1996-1997 winter season
- The least number of U.S. blizzards in a season: was 1, during the 1980-1981 winter season
- The average population affected per blizzard was 2.5 million
- The peak month is January overall, noting regional differences

In addition, within this region of high blizzard activity, each state has a history of notable blizzard-related events that supports the study's findings. Among the history of states within this high-blizzard activity region, notable winter events include:

Minnesota
The earliest recorded blizzard for Minnesota s was from 1866. According to the Minnesota Climatology Working Group, this first recorded blizzard was among the worst. It was said to have lasted for 3 days, and resulted in 20 foot (over 6 meters) high snowdrifts. Blizzards in Minnesota are particularly brutal. A blizzard in 1888 was responsible for killing some killed 200 people. The so-called "Armistice Day Blizzard" of 1940[11] was responsible for an estimated 100 deaths. Finally, in 1975, more

---

[10] Schwartz, Robert M., Thomas W. Schmidlin, 2002: Climatology of Blizzards in the Conterminous United States, 1959–2000. J. Climate, 15, 1765–1772.

14 people died because of blizzard-like conditions, with another 21 more dying of heart attacks during and after the storm passed.

South Dakota
South Dakota too is known for extreme blizzards. In 1975, a blizzard dumped a relatively paltry amount of snow—just 7 inches (17 centimeters)—on much of the state. However, along with the blizzard came winds of 70 mph (112 km/h), creating a wind chill factor of minus 70 degrees Fahrenheit (-56 Celsius). Visibility during the height of the storm was limited to less than 1/4th of a mile (402 meters) for a full day, and caused 8 deaths. Finally, a freak blizzard in October of 2013 came on the heels of 70 and 80 (F) degree days (21 and 26 C.). The relative sudden and un-forecasted blizzard caused the deaths of between 7,000 and 100,000 head of cattle and other livestock.

North Dakota
Blizzards that strike North Dakota tend to originate with weather patterns that form either over the southern part of the Canadian province of Alberta, or over the state of Colorado. Because of this, weather systems that form blizzards over North Dakota are called "Alberta-"and/or "Colorado-Lows." This unique "either-or" climatic setup poses more of a blizzard threat because these storms tend develop more rapidly. This dynamic was observed in March 1941 when the state (along with northern parts of Minnesota) was suddenly struck by an intense blizzard. On March 15th—without warning—the storm swept in from west of the state, causing temperatures to drop 20 degrees in less than 15 minutes. Winds from the sudden store exceeded 50 mph (more than 80 km/h), with gusts reaching at least 85 mph (135 km/h) in the city of Grand Forks. Between the suddenness of the storm, the fast-dropping extreme temperatures, the blinding snow, and the 7 feet (over 2 meters) high snow drifts left in the blizzard's wake, a total of 151 people would perish from the disaster.

Outside of this "blizzard alley," these winter storms can be just as severe...and extensive. Blizzards in the New England area typify this. Among the most notable was Blizzard of 1978, which struck areas of the American Northeast between February 5th and 7th of that year. During the height of the catastrophic blizzard, all but necessary emergency activity was halted by the storm's presence, including mail delivery—which rarely is ever affected by events. Many cities and towns in the region broke snowfall accumulation records, some of which still stand currently. The storm killed approximately 100 people, injured more than 4,500 others, and was responsible for more than half a billion dollars in damage and lost economic activity (equivalent to about $520 1.86 billion in today's dollar amounts).

The New England area of the U.S. is unique in that it also experiences—in addition to blizzards—a unique type of storm known as a *nor'easter blizzard*. A nor'easter blizzard, so-named because of the general direction from which the winds produced by these storms blow, describes a circulating system of low-pressure which has a center of rotation that is usually located along or just off the Eastern Coast of the country. During a nor'easter blizzard, the leading winds are found in the left-forward quadrant of the storm's rotation, which tends to produce high winds, heavy snow, and cold temperatures over the land areas it affects.

---

[11] The Armistice Day Blizzard of 1940 was a 1,000 mile (1600 km) -wide storm track that raged across the Midwest region of the U.S. on November 11th and 13th of that year. Over this 2-day period, the storm caused an estimated $2-million dollars in damage (in 1940 value amounts, equivalent to about 35-million in today's dollars), and was responsible for more than 140 deaths in 6 different states: Nebraska, South Dakota, Iowa, Minnesota, Wisconsin, and Michigan.

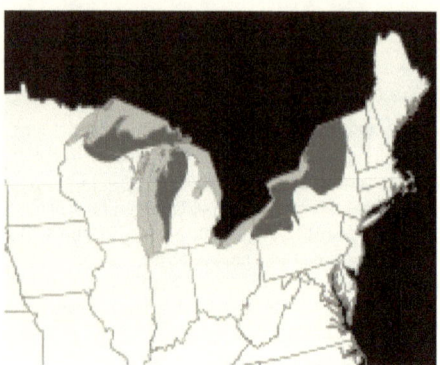

The established lake-effect snow belts around the various Great Lakes. In heavy lake-effect snow events, the snow often affects areas miles/kilometers away from the immediate snow belt areas, depending on the directions of the winds fueling the lake-effect snows.

Areas in and around the region of the U.S.' Great Lakes, known collectively as "the lake-effect snow belts" are also more prone to blizzards. The lake-effect snow belts are areas of the country, primarily[12] consisting of several regions near the Great Lakes that tend to experience greater amounts of accumulated snow than the rest of the country due to the regular occurrence of sometimes heavy lake-effect snows. Sometimes within these snow belts, *lake-effect blizzards* form. These are—for want of a better term—"mini-blizzards." That result from heavy lake-effect snow events. These events may be accompanied by exceptionally strong winds, creating blizzard-like conditions. However, there are 3 major differences between lake-effect blizzards and general blizzards, the first being that general blizzards tend form from established weather systems. Another difference between the two is that lake-effect blizzards tend to cover more area than a ground blizzard, but less than a general blizzard, which is more widespread. Finally, lake-effect blizzards are usually of a shorter than that of a general blizzard (which is why general blizzard warnings are not issued by authorities in this case).

---

[12] The Great Salt Lake in the state of Utah is the only other lake that produces significant lake effect snow in the United States.

The No-Nonsense Guide To Blizzard Safety

What to Be On the Alert for...

Blizzards, unlike most other natural disasters tend to have fewer general variations between them, outside of wind speed and duration of each storm. For the most part, all blizzards tend to have some level of snowfall that is often blown about by high winds to the point where visibility becomes an immediate hazard. Most take place in the winter months, although there are some instances where a few blizzards have struck in the earliest part of the spring and late fall months.

During these particular times of the year (the winter months and the transitional periods before and after winter) keeping abreast of rapidly-changing weather should command at least some attention. Most weather forecasts will provide a fairly accurate multi-day projection of conditions for a given period of weather-related activity, including winter-related periods. To this effect, meteorologists are able to project with a moderate to accurate degree of certainty the gathering conditions for blizzards. When these conditions appear likely, weather forecasters will issue the appropriate weather advisories to the public.

In the U.S., a *blizzard watch* will be issued by the National Weather Service (NWS)—an arm of the federal government—between 12 and 48 hours prior to the onset of blizzards conditions (just as in other countries around the globe, similarly responsible government agencies will issue similar advisories. In Canada for example, weather advisories will be issued by Environment Canada). When a blizzard watch is issued, it generally means that forecasters are at least 50% certain that a blizzard event is about to occur. Depending on changing conditions, a blizzard watch will either be downgraded or updated. [13]

In the case of upgrading weather advisories due to worsening conditions, a *blizzard warning* will be issued by the NWS. A blizzard warning is meant to convey that—at the very least—the conditions of a minimal blizzard are imminent within the next 12 to 24 hours. In cases when the projected weather conditions will significantly exceed the minimal threshold for a blizzard, a severe blizzard warning will be issued. During a severe blizzard (warning), areas can expect winds exceeding 45 mph (72 km/h), and temperatures extremes of below 10°F (-12°C). In either case, local weather offices will broadcast advisories and/or alarms over the National Oceanic and Atmospheric Administration (NOAA) weather radio frequencies, while making automated voice broadcasts warnings of deteriorating weather conditions. Areas and regions under a blizzard warning can usually expect heavy falling and wind-driven snow, strong winds, near zero visibility, deep drifts, and life-threatening wind chills. However, weather forecasting is not infallible insofar as its accuracy.

There are times when suddenly-changing conditions might defy the best attempts to provide accurate forecasting, such as in the case of the sudden October 2013 blizzard that raged through parts of South Dakota (page 15). During such times, there are usually weather-related indicators that point to the imminent arrival of blizzard conditions, even outside of projected weather forecasts. This is why vigilance and observation are such important components in preparing for disasters such as blizzards. If one is observant, they will notice a change in wind patterns as well as the overall strength of the wind. Increased winds prior to a blizzard will almost always be accompanied by a significant drop in

---

[13] There are several different weather advisories related to winter weather that the NWS will issue, depending on snow total projections and accompanying conditions. For a list of these different weather advisories , as well as their forecast effects , see Appendix: A in the back of the book.

temperatures (or the temperature drop may in fact, begin *before* an increase in wind speeds). In some cases, dark gray low-hanging clouds will gather prior to the start of heavy snow. If snow begins falling consistently and clouds still appear heavy, a blizzard is much more likely.

There is also anecdotal evidence suggesting that the behavior of animals tends to change with the imminent arrival of a disaster or serious change in weather. The assumption is that animals can sense weather changes and vibrations in the earth that human beings are unable to, outside of the use of complex instrumentation. Many farmers are said to embrace observing animal behavior as an indicator of oncoming inclimate weather such blizzards with some level of reliability. For example, it's believed that the absence of birds on particular trees where they would normally be found perching for no apparent reason would be a reliable indicator of a blizzard. Another observation related to birds and oncoming adverse weather [disasters] is that the flying patterns of birds tend to change when they apparently sense a change in conditions. Birds will often fly lower in the sky before a snowstorm/blizzard where they would normally been seen flying higher.

Insomuch as other animal behavior that might be considered unusual in advance of a blizzard, animals such as rabbits and chipmunks are said to often avoid leaving their burrows. Although this phenomenon of "strange" animal behavior as an indicator of a change in weather patterns is being studied by some scientists, others such as farmers tend to swear by these "markers" of imminent bad weather as being reliable. Although it may or may not have some credence, in the end it may be best to rely on one's own observations to determine whether or not a blizzard may be in the future.

The No-Nonsense Guide To Blizzard Safety

How to Prepare In The Event Of a Blizzard...

   As with any natural disaster or weather extreme of some level of probability, the best way to prepare for a blizzard is to be proactive. Anyone who lives in a region where blizzards are an irregular (or regular) occurrence should have not only a prepared plan of action for getting through this particular weather-related crisis, but *should* have protocols in place in the event that they are caught in a less-than-desirable position during a blizzard.

Before a Blizzard
   Blizzards are extreme winter storms capable of causing loss of electrical power, heat, and telephone service. What's more, these storms have the potential to actually trap individuals in their homes if they are accompanied by exceedingly high snow amounts (this is because heavy snow can not only pack snow high enough on the ground to potentially block windows and doors, but the addition of the high winds can create even higher snow drifts...further blocking any exits and entrances). Even in less worse-case scenarios, driveways, streets, and other main roadway arteries can be blocked for days, further potentially trapping those who might be affected. For this reason, it's important that homes and other potential places of refuge in a blizzard have ample supplies at hand in preparation for the possibility that travel outside the place of refuge may be hindered for an extended period.
   Homes and other lodgings should be winterized. Water pipes should be insulated against falling temperatures outside. Many hardware stores offer pipe wrapping for sale, which prevents running water from freezing inside of pipes and disrupting the water supply (this also prevents water pipes from freezing, which could cause them to potentially burst). Tree branches near homes and buildings that could break off and/or fall onto these dwellings should be either trimmed of cut, as they could easily be torn off by the high winds a blizzard produces. Commodities that serve as sources of heat such as heating oil, firewood, propane, etc. should be re-stocked and checked to ensure an ample supply for an extended period. Additionally, all seals in and around doors and window should be sealed to keep out cold air drafts. The best way to accomplish this is to apply weather-stripping to doors and windows (this can be purchased in the form of adhesive narrow strips from any hardware or home-improvement stores). The caulking of any air gaps via cracks or holes should also be undertaken to keep heat from escaping.[14] Installing and/or replacing the batteries in carbon monoxide detectors should also be a priority, especially in winter months when malfunctions of furnaces and other heating sources could cause the buildup of deadly carbon monoxide gas[15].
   And just as one should prepare a stockpile of anticipated supplies in preparation for the aftermath of other related weather events (like tornadoes and hurricanes), those living in areas prone to blizzards should consider gather necessary supplies and equipment that may lesson any inconveniences and/or

---

[14] Air pockets and gaps in buildings and homes can be located in several different ways. One of the easiest ways is to use a cigarette lighter or a lit candle to walk around suspected areas of drafts. A flame flickering in one direction is an indication that air may be coming into the home through a nearby crack or hole. An object that produces a steady stream of smoke or visible vapor such as a lit incense stick has the same effect of locating drafts and air pockets.

[15] Carbon monoxide (or CO) is an odorless, colorless gas naturally produced by the combustion of burning fuels. CO is most often produced by—among other things—vehicles, small gasoline engines, stoves, lanterns, burning charcoal and wood, and home/building heating systems. CO, if allowed to accumulate in spaces without the proper ventilation (such as enclosed rooms), can result in *carbon monoxide poisoning* for people (or animals) breathing in CO fumes. Moderately prolonged inhalation of CO causes loss of consciousness and eventual death, as CO replaces oxygen in the bloodstream of those affected by carbon monoxide poisoning.

disruption of utility services. This may be done either by purchasing a *blizzard survival kit* (many of which can be purchased online), or building one piecemeal. Among the essential supplies a blizzard survival kit should contain are:

Foodstuffs (at least a 3-day supply of each)

- Bottled water (in the event that pipes become frozen and well inoperable). In addition, any pets and infants should have their own supply of water as well.
- Non-perishable foods. Foods that require little or no preparation (i.e., no cooking) are best. This would include dried fruit, protein and/or high-energy bars/granola bars, canned goods, dried/canned meats, crackers, nuts, and/or similarly low/no-preparation foods. Additionally, such items should have an extended shelf-life, so as to limit the possibility that they may not be edible in the event of need.
- Powdered milk and/or fruit juices.

Communication equipment

- A battery-powered NOAA weather radio/battery-powered portable radio/television to receive emergency information.
- A cell-phone, preferably one with internet access (along with an extra battery, fully charged). Depending on the circumstances, this may be the only link to the outside world should access roads become inaccessible. I list of emergency contacts should be programmed into the phone's electronic directory.

Other-related supplies/miscellaneous

- A manual can opener.
- Extra batteries (for battery-powered equipment).
- A snow shovel (preferably more than one), or a gas-powered snow blower.
- Rock salt or snow-melt (to assist in clearing snow).
- Flashlights, candles, or another source of light in the event that power is loss.
- A basic first-aid kit (purchased or created).
- "Canned-heat," a source of cooking fuel if power or gas utilities are disrupted. This item can be purchased at a camping supply store or in a department retail outlet.
- Extra blankets and/or sleeping bags (for extra warmth should power supplies be disrupted).

Along with preparing supplies, extra [warm] clothing should also be readily assessable in the event that heating is disrupted. A common closet within the home should be a designated and generally understood place to store a bag of warm clothing for each person in the household. In the event of a power loss, common knowledge of this closet's location will make it easier to locate extra clothing if needed.

Becoming stranded in an automobile during a blizzard is a distinct possibility during the winter, especially in blizzard-prone regions. Because of this very real possibility, it might be prudent to winterize and prepare any owned automobiles in the same way one would prepare their homes. This is to say that vehicles should be stockpiled with a level of anticipated supplies equal to that one would similarly stockpile in a home. And since those travelling in vehicles are far more vulnerable to being affected by the extreme conditions of blizzards, it may be even more important to prepare vehicles for this contingency than homes. A blizzard survival kit for an automobile should contain much of the following supplies:

- A cell phone, preferably one with texting capabilities, as well as a cell phone charger (of course one would not want to text while driving. However, at times when receiving a wireless signal by cell phone can be difficult should one become stranded in an isolated location, most times it is far easier for a text message to make it through to others when making calls for assistance is more difficult. Text messages have the added advantage of not "breaking up" in the same way that calls do).
- At least 2 blankets and/or sleeping bags (to maintain warmth).
- A flashlight, with extra batteries.
- A utility tool, such as a Swiss knife.
- High calorie, non-perishable food items, such as protein/cereal bars, dried jerky, or other such foods with long-term storage capacity.
- A case of bottled water.
- A small shovel.
- Sand or cat litter (to provide traction in extricating vehicles should a vehicle becomes stuck in snow
- A windshield scraper (with a brush to brush off snow).
- A tool kit
- Jumper cables or a charging unit.[16]
- A paper roadmap, compass, and/or a GPS unit.
- A tow rope or chain (in the event that the vehicle needs to be pulled out from snow by another vehicle).
- An extra change of clothes, or additional winter gear (such as boots, heavy socks, gloves, and/or another coat).
- Tissue or toilet paper.

Furthermore, vehicles with an expected use for travel during winter months—especially in heavily inclimate weather regions—should maintain a full tank of fuel. This limits the likelihood that travelers might in fact become stranded, as well as prevents a vehicle's fuel line from freezing.

Although storing these vital supplies in a vehicle for possible use is a good start, it's *still* necessary to winterize vehicles in much the same way that homes should be winterized against harsh weather. Tires used during other times of the year should be replaced with either snow tires (which are made

---

[16] A charging unit is a portable device used in the event providing a starting charge for vehicle batteries that cannot provide enough of an electrical spark to start a vehicle. Most require prior charging from a household outlet for a number of hours before use.

especially for harsher winter weather), or all-weather tires. The various necessary engine fluids—particularly antifreeze—should be changed, refilled, and/or replaced prior to winter/blizzard conditions setting in; the various belts and other high turn-over parts should also be inspected and replaced as needed (in many cases, reputable repair and auto maintenance shops will perform inspections of these components either free of charge, or for a nominal fee). Finally, vehicles should also receive engine tune-ups at least twice a year, and fueled levels should be kept at ample supply levels as to prevent running out at a critical juncture in inclimate weather.

And while venturing outdoors during a blizzard is **not advised**, there may be cases such as emergencies when doing so may become necessary. If going outdoors or travelling during a blizzard becomes necessary, then the proper clothing is essential to prevent the onset of health issues such as hypothermia or frostbite—as well as to simply stay warm during these harsh weather conditions. Rather than opting to wear a single layer of heavy clothing, wearing several layers of warm lightweight, loose-fitting clothing works best. In addition to helping to maintain body heat, multiple layers of lighter clothing has the added advantage of ease in adding or removing more layers as the conditions and locations change. The removal of clothing layers may become necessary to avoid overheating, perspiration, and any subsequent chill. The outermost garments of winter dress should be of a tightly-woven material (such as duck or twill), or consist of water-repellant material. As for the hands, mittens tend to be a better choice than gloves, as they force the fingers to be in close proximity to each other, making better use of the body's heating. The head should always be covered during cold weather; wearing a hat or head covering conserves more body heat. During strong blizzards, or conditions when the wind chill (or actual air temperature) is well below freezing, covering the mouth with a facemask or scarf will protect the lungs from the effects of the extremely cold air. Lastly, well-insulated waterproof boots will work to keep the feet from becoming wet from the snow, which otherwise would increase the risk for frostbite.

Outside of emergency plans, information is the biggest advantage one can own in planning for blizzards as well as other disasters and emergencies. Insomuch as blizzards are concerned, the basis of the information should be to know when blizzard conditions are likely or imminent. Always monitor the weather during inclimate or adverse weather conditions. Doing so will allow those who might be affected by such dangerous weather to make informed decisions about any planned course of action. Having a radio or television close at-hand may keep someone from venturing out in weather that could result in a potential loss of life and/or limb.

During a Blizzard

It's the worst-case scenario; a blizzard is imminent or is occurring. However, the keys to managing any crisis like a blizzard are planning and information. But if contingency plans are followed, and maintaining access to information is kept consistent both prior to and during the event, a blizzard could turn out to be an easily-managed crisis. First and foremost, know what the weather conditions are prior to planning any activity which in weather might be a factor. Know that travelling in extreme conditions such as blizzards has many dangers, and is highly discouraged. Paying heed to weather advisories and/or warnings should be taken seriously, as to limit the chance that one might find themselves trapped outdoors in a blizzard.

However, nature at times has its own designs and timetables, and it is entirely possible—despite knowing projected weather forecasts—that one might find themselves unexpectantly caught in a blizzard. The first rule in any crisis situation is **don't panic!** In most emergencies, both common sense and the need for clear-thinking apply. Should anyone find themselves either travelling through or caught unawares in a vehicle during a blizzard, drivers should slow down, and drive with their hazard lights activated. The blinking lights will alert other drivers to the hazardous conditions as well as enable others to see the vehicle.

In some cases, conditions may deteriorate to the point where driving may become too dangerous to continue. In other cases, stopped automobiles may stall, stranding travelers. In the event that travelers should become snowbound in their vehicles, consider the following guidelines to keep safe and increase odds of survival:

- If travelling by car becomes necessary, it should be done so during the daylight hours only (if possible). Also, travelling should also not be undertaken alone; drivers should take at least one other person on any extended trip in adverse winter conditions. Driving should also be limited to main roads and/or heavily travelled arteries, while informing others before leaving, and upon arrival to the destination (in fact, others should be made aware of the route to be travelled and the approximate schedule of travelling time).
- Vehicles should pull off the road/over to the side of the road and the vehicle's hazard lights activated (to both make the vehicle more visible in the reduce visibility conditions as well as indicate distress).
- Any distressed vehicles can be made more noticeable to passersby and potential rescuers. If driving at night, the interior dome light should be turned on (but *only when the vehicle's engine is running*, otherwise keeping the light on may run down the battery's power reserves). Consider tying a brightly colored piece of cloth or other object to the vehicles antenna or someplace on the vehicle where it might capture attention. Finally, raising the hood of the vehicle projects distress (but do so only *after* the snows has stopped falling and/or blowing).
- Occupants should stay inside the vehicle (to prevent venturing out in the extreme conditions, in which it is very easy to become disoriented by the blinding snow and wind). Walking in a blizzard is not advisable, and should only be attempted if assistance is relatively close by (e.g., if a building is within walking distance where those in the vehicle can either secure assistance of take shelter in).
- In cases where it applies, the vehicle should be turned off to preserve fuel (i.e., where vehicles are still operable). The vehicle's motor should be turned on for about 10-minutes every hour to generate heat.
- Windows should be opened slightly to prevent the buildup of carbon monoxide vapors (this is especially true if snow builds up to the point where a vehicle's exhaust is confined or even blocked by high snow drifts. Any snow that is found blocking the vehicle's exhaust pipe should be removed).
- Movements such as calisthenics (e.g., exercise) generate body heat. Frequently engaging in such movements also keeps the blood circulating in the body. Clapping hands, stomping feet, and moving around at moderate levels of activity are advised. And while all such activity is

highly encouraged, avoid overexertion and potentially working up a sweat (moisture on the surface of the skin can actually make feel colder under such conditions). In addition, consider huddling with other passengers in the vehicle. Huddling takes advantage of multiple individuals' body heat by the sharing close physical proximity. Any available coats should be as a blanket (for extra insulation). In extreme cold, the use of paper road maps, seat covers, floor mats, newspapers, and/ or extra clothing is highly encouraged in order to provide additional insulation and warmth.

Once the blizzard is over, it may be safer for occupants to exit the vehicle and proceed walking to secure assistance. If walking does becomes necessary, a path that follows the same general direction of the road is the best route; following the road itself (without walking too close to it) is the best choice. If forced to walk across open country or rural areas, distant points should be used as landmarks to help maintain a general sense of direction sense of direction.

On this particular note, in the event that one finds themselves outdoors during a blizzard, the same first rule of *don't panic* still applies. The first priority for anyone in such a position is to locate shelter from the elements, particularly the storm's frigid winds. Blowing winds can cause the wind chill to reduce the body's core temperature to dangerous levels, and the earliest effects of frostbite could begin setting in as little as 10-minutes if shelter isn't sought or found immediately. If an automobile is available, protection from the wind should be sought there (following the suggestions listed on page 23). In urban areas, service/gas stations (which are usually open under most cases), places of public accommodation (i.e., municipal building, public library, or store), and/or private businesses not only provide protection from the wind, but are usually warm. If none of these are available, it may become necessary to improvise a shelter. Public bus stops (those that are semi – or fully-enclosed), garages, tool sheds, or even abandoned buildings are places to consider in such an instance.

In rural areas, the situation becomes more of a crisis, as dwellings usually found in abundance in urban areas are less common in these areas. While finding shelter from the wind and cold should still be the first priority in such a situation, being able to improvise is even more imperative to ensure one's well-being should one finds themselves caught in a blizzard. If a sturdy shelter such as a building is unavailable, the priority then shifts to staying as dry as possible while searching for shelter. All exposed parts of the body should be protected by some form of wrapping, or even just simply using the arms and hands (such as using the hands to shield one's face). If possible, light a fire to stay warm, and to dry wet clothing while using any available material for kindling. Rocks, stones, or some other fire-resistance materials and/or objects should be placed around any fire to help absorb and reflect heat. Fire also has the added benefit of attracting the attention of would-be rescuers.

If building a fire is not an option, then the best course of action among limited options is to take advantage of the snow itself. Deep snow can actually act as an insulator from the wind and cold temperatures, a fact that is well-known and best exemplified by the Inuit people of Canada's Arctic regions (the Inuit, formerly known as "Eskimos," have been using snow to insulate their igloo homes for centuries). In the case of being stranded in a blizzard, carving out an improvised shelter out of snow can be potentially life-saving. A snow-cave can be carved out of snow drifts/accumulated snow to provide protection from the winds, and serve as a temporary place of refuge until the worst of the storm passes by. Similarly, a large piece of plywood, cardboard, bundled sticks (of approximately the same size and/or length), or a large piece of fabric (such as a plastic tarp) can be fashioned together to create a lean-to, serving as a windbreak.

During periods when one might be stranded, particularly in a snowstorm, maintaining optimal health for as long as possible is a key in order to see a crisis through to the end. To this end, staying hydrated is a major component of this imperative. Finding a source of water is important during these times, and the snow itself should serve as the source should bottled water not be available. However, eating snow is not advised. Doing so will lower the body's temperature (and increasing the risk for hypothermia). Snow should be melted before being consumed for water. The best way to accomplish this is to gather snow in a container of some sort of container. The snow should either be placed next to a heat source such as a flame, or kept close to the body (utilizing the body's heat to speed up the melting process).

The image on the left is an example of an emergency snow cave shelter, carved out of a snow bank. The right image is an example of a lean-to composed of cut tree branches, twigs, and sticks. In the example of the lean-to, the "roof" can be substituted for a single piece object such as a large piece of cardboard of plywood.

Finally, if one is fortunate enough to be in a home or building during a blizzard, the best advice is to **stay inside.** If adverse weather conditions are expected to go on for an extended period, both heat and fuel should be conserved—especially in rural areas where it is easier to become snowbound. If possible, heating to less-used or unused rooms should be limited or temporarily shut off altogether until the need to conserve passes. The use of fire safeguards when using alternative sources of heating (e.g., a wood-burning stove, space heater, of a fireplace) is highly advised in order to prevent the possibility of hire resulting from the attempt to stay warm. Additionally, the use ample ventilation is critical when using kerosene-fueled heaters in order to avoid the buildup of toxic fumes (i.e., carbon monoxide). If space heaters require refueling, this should be done in a well-ventilated area away from the living quarters or areas where others are congregating; refuel space heaters on an enclosed porch or even outside close to the home/building. It's a good idea that space heaters of all types be kept at least 3 feet (about a single meter) from flammable objects while operating.

In the event that electricity (and in many cases, heat as a result) is disrupted, remaining calm is the best option. In most instances, power loss is a temporary inconvenience at best; eventually, the power (and heat) will be return. At this point, the primary goal is to retain as much of the warm in the home/building as possible. Closing off uninhibited rooms, and stuffing towels or rags in the cracks under the entrances to these rooms is an excellent starting point. If possible, all inhabitants should gather in one or two rooms to take advantage of shared body heat generated by multiple individuals in enclosed spaces. If the power/heat loss takes place at night, windows should be covered with towels of some other light barrier to help preserve heat. All occupants should stay nourished, eating high-energy food to help the body stay healthy and generate its own heat. All occupants should also replenish with fluids in order to prevent dehydration. During this time, maintaining spirits and providing distractions from any stress produced by the ordeal should be kept to minimum. Parlor games and reading material are excellent ways to reduce stress (although cell phones should not be used to play games, as their use might be required should an emergency arises).

In the most extreme circumstances, such as an extended period of heat and/or power loss, consider relocating to established and/or designated public shelters. Such an option should also be considered if supplies run out during an extended blizzard. [17]

After the Blizzard

After the winds have died down and the snow stops falling and blowing, it's a probable sign that a blizzard has passed. During this time, it may be safe to venture outside to engage in a general well-being check of property as well as assess general conditions. During this time, it might be a good idea to inspect the home/building for any damage that may have occurred to its structure. Also, consider checking in on neighbors to ensure that no one needs emergency assistance. Run water and flush toilets to ensure that pipes are not frozen and/or obstructed. If water/plumbing pipes are frozen, using a blow dryer to heat the pipe at the suspected point of obstruction may melt the ice-clog. A space heater placed in front of an open bathroom vanity or kitchen sink cabinet can be used to thaw pipes under a sink. For more serious obstructions, it may be necessary to either contact a plumber or wait for roadways to be plowed before attempting to make related purchases to remedy the problem.

In the most extreme cases, blizzards and related conditions may have catastrophic-level impact on a region. This was seen during the so-called "Storm of the Century" that occurred in 1993, affecting nearly the entire eastern seaboard of the U.S as well as the island of Cuba and parts of Southern Canada. Though not technically a blizzard, the *'93 Superstorm* (as it was also called) was a cyclonic storm that formed over the Gulf of Mexico, and eventually merged with other existing weather patterns to form a unique and intense center of circulation reminiscent of a traditional nor'easter. This resulting cyclonic storm produced tornado-spawning supercell thunderstorms in the state of Florida, record sea-tides in the Gulf of Mexico, plummeting temperature in the country's Northeast and parts of the South,[18] and record snowfalls and blizzards in the Mid-South and Eastern parts of the country. The result was over 300 deaths overall, structural damage to buildings and homes in the affected area that included collapsed roofs, and the complete economic shutdown of areas under the storm's impact. In such rare

---

[17] **Know when to go to a shelter.** In the event that conditions in the home become unbearable or causes undue risks, The Federal Emergency Management Agency (FEMA) operates a phone-based database of local emergency shelters. Local shelters can be located by texting SHELTER + your ZIP code to 43352 (4FEMA) by cell phone. FEMA will respond by text with the location of the nearest shelter.

[18] In the days and weeks immediately prior to the development of the 1993 *Superstorm*, temperatures accompanying the storm were typical for early spring in the parts of the country affected by the storm, between46 °F (8 °C) and 65 °F (18 °C), depending on the state and location. During the 1993 storm, many affected locations were all below freezing. In fact, parts of New England saw daily maximum temperatures as low as 14 °F (−10 °C).

and extreme instances, federal assistance may be required. This is especially true when local resources are limited and/or nonexistent, such as it was in parts of the American South in the immediate days after the 1993 storm.[19] In such cases, the Federal Emergency Management Agency (FEMA) may become involved in recovery and/or cleanup undertakings.[20]

Clearing or less adverse conditions is the best time to attempt to engage in snow removal responsibilities. When either operating a snow blower or shoveling snow, it is imperative to pace one's self. The combination of overexertion and cold temperatures could increase the both the chances and risk of a heart attacks while attempting to remove snow. Also, take advantage of natural heat of the sun; try shoveling to a point (i.e., not a complete snow removal) where the sun's heat can melt what's left of the snow (assuming of course, that skies have cleared). Removing snow from sidewalks and stairs will allow any post-blizzard sunlight to warm up the pavement underneath. This also prevents ice from forming and creating hazards for those walking by (in many localities in the U.S., ordinances mandate that sidewalks in front of homes be void of snow to aid in the delivery of mail and other necessary services). Another option to help eliminate accumulated snow is the use of chemical snow removers. Salt-based compounds may be used to help speed up the melting icy patches[21]. To optimize these substances to their maximum efficiency, it is best to apply them on snow-covered sidewalks overnight to prevent melting snow from refreezing.

Finally, while outdoors, it is important to monitor the health of those involved in snow-removal. Those engaged in physical activities should watch for any indication of declining health, such as the early signs of frostbite and hypothermia. These include the loss of feeling in the arms and legs, uncontrolled shivering, slurred speech, and disorientation/dizziness. Additionally, looking out for the signs of a heart attack is also encouraged; sweating, difficulty breathing/shortness of breath, nausea, pressure, tightness, pain, and/or a squeezing or aching sensation in the chest or arms that may spread to the neck, jaw or back should be particularly noted and taken seriously.

Limiting exposure to the wind and cold during (and after) a blizzard is the primary goal, while seeking or maintaining shelter as the means to this end is the secondary goal. Whether indoors, traveling by (or stranded in a) vehicle, or outdoors, the purpose of planning and acting on those plans is to limit the effect of crisis moments created by blizzards. Effective planning allow individuals to wait out a blizzard if indoors, to outlast an active blizzard long enough for travel to a place of shelter (if stranded in a vehicle), or remain active (and alive) long enough to be located by rescuers (if outdoors or on foot.). In either case, avoiding the common urge to panic during an overwhelming crisis—while focusing on the task of ensuring one's personal well-being through an emergency situation—can increase the likelihood of seeing the end of any crisis related to blizzards.

---

[19] In many areas of the America South, the lack of yearly significant snowfall has developed into a general policy where many local public works departments (at the local and state levels) simply do not devote any significant portion of their budgets and material to snow removal.

[20] See Appendix: B in the rear of the rear of the book for a listing of FEMA regional offices and contact information.

[21] In using chemical snow removers, it should be noted that these compounds effectiveness in melting snow diminishes with colder temperatures. Starting at around 15 to 20 F (-9 to -6 C), the melting properties of chemical snow removers becomes hindered. The closer the temperatures get to 0 F (-17 C), the less impact such substances have on snow. However, the temperature of the pavement beneath the snow can be a factor in using these products. A warmer pavement temperature (warmer than the air temperature) can maintain the effect of snow-melting chemicals at temperatures that would normally be ineffective if the chemicals were placed directly on the snot itself with no pavement exposed.

The No-Nonsense Guide To Blizzard Safety

What to Avoid

Just as there are for any natural (or manmade) disaster, precautions and planning can limit the possibility of both injury and/or death to those individuals such events might affect. Bad decisions, bad planning, and panicking are sure-fire ways to increase the likelihood of harm during blizzards. Such counter-productive undertakings will invariably lead to counter-productive actions. Among the actions that one should avoid prior to, and during a blizzard are:

- Not planning ahead. In most things that matter, preparation is always better than chance. Stocking up on supplies, preparing automobiles for winter weather, and having access to information such as weather reports can save a life during blizzard events.
- Under-dressing for the weather. Assuming that brief warm spells, especially during the winter months will last for an extended period of time can lead one into a false sense of security. Not dressing appropriately for the proper time of year can lead to one being caught unawares should the weather changes. Under-dressing in cold temperatures can potentially lead to hypothermia and/or frostbite.
- Traveling during blizzards and severe winter storms. Even the most experienced drivers are vulnerable to the effects of extreme weather as it affects visibility, steering control, and traction. Between these hazards, the extreme temperatures, and the presence of other drivers, it is simply not worth tempting fate to attempt to drive during such conditions.

Summary

Because blizzards and other severe winter storms occur every year around the world, individuals can either be marginally inconvenienced, or significantly impacted—depending on the extent and severity of a particular storm. Issues created by blizzards include the inability to travel from one location to another because of closed roads, and potentially affected daily economic activity in the affected area. Additionally, electrical outages are also prevalent during winter snow storms and blizzards.

Preparation for winter storms is necessary to ensure that daily life is only minimally affected, and to ensure the well-being of those who might experience these storms. Successful preparations to consider include the creation of an emergency plan, adequate supplies, including fuels, foodstuffs, and water for a 3-day period. In most cases, blizzards and severe winter storms are best ridden out by sheltering in place during the storm, and attempting to go out only after the storm has ended.

In general, rural areas tend to be more susceptible to power outages and the most negative effects of blizzards than urban areas. Also, rural locations are more likely to experience livestock and economic issues related to agriculture as negative impacts of blizzards, while urban areas are impacted by the cost of impeded commerce, transportation, and property damage (e.g., automobiles and other property damaged by traffic accidents).

In addition to property and economic damage, blizzards are "silent killers." Health issues such as heart attacks are not commonly thought to be related, but nevertheless impacts individuals every year as they are forced to cope with the affects of blizzards. What's more, the effects and extent of other related health issues such as potential frostbite and hypothermia are generally undetected until after the danger has passed—and the opportunity to examine those affected presents itself. Taken altogether, the hazards and dangers created by blizzards—both the obvious and not so obvious hazards—should not be underestimated in the least.

Points To Remember

- Information is the best asset in any potential disaster situation, including blizzards. It is important to have and monitor a weather radio. In the absence of a weather radio, access to local television, radio, or an internet feed that broadcasts local weather reports is necessary in order to be kept abreast of impending adverse weather conditions and vital updates from the National Weather Service (NWS).
- In addition to insulating pipes, another way to keep water from freezing inside them is to run a constant trickle of water during a blizzard. This keeps water circulating through pipes and limits the chance that any residual water from freezing, causing a blockage and/or rupturing the pipes. Opening kitchen and bathroom cabinet doors will allow warmer air to circulate around the plumbing, further limiting the chance that pipes may freeze.
- All fuel-burning equipment should be operated away from flammable objects and/or substances, and in a well-ventilated area.
- All holes, cracks, seams, and other openings should be sealed to keep heat inside and cold air outside as temperatures drop.
- Conserve heat and fuel during colder temperatures. Thermostat settings should remain constant throughout the duration of the blizzard, both day and night. This not only conserves fuel, but lowers the likelihood that pipes will freeze up during the night.
- Pets and/or animal companion should be brought indoors prior to the arrival of a blizzard or severe winter weather. Other animals and/or or livestock should be sheltered in areas with unhindered access to food and water.
- **Stay indoors and restrict travel to emergencies only**. Travelling should be limited to emergency situations only. If venturing outdoors, wearing warm, loose-fitting, lightweight clothing in several layers offers protection from possible frostbite and hypothermia.
- Vehicles should be prepared for hazardous winter weather. Changing fluids, tires, belts, and packing an emergency kit in a vehicle limits the chance(s) of becoming stranded in a blizzard while ensuring a traveler's well-being should they actually become stranded. Maintaining a full fuel tank at all times while driving in a cautious manner further limits the possibility of being stranded in an automobile. Also, avoid driving when conditions include sleet, freezing rain or drizzle, snow or dense fog.
- In the event that any power and/or heating loss to a home is expected to go on for extended periods [of extreme cold] during a blizzard, preparations should be made to relocate to a local designated public shelter.
- Before tackling strenuous tasks in cold temperatures, individuals should consider their physical condition, the outside temperature, and the nature (i.e., the demands) of the task at hand.

- Individuals including elderly people living alone, people with disabilities and children require special assistance. Remember to make special provisions for such special-needs individuals when making emergency plans.

Notes

Blizzard History

The following blizzard-related events are notable for the particular extreme weather records they produced, as well as providing an illustration of the varying impact and effects these extreme winter storms represent.

Date	Location	Impact/Significance
February 1972	Northwest regions of Iran	The Iran Blizzard of February 1972 holds the record for being the deadliest blizzard in recorded history. The storm resulted in the deaths of approximately 4,000 people. A week-long period of low temperatures and were hardest hit, with no survivors in Kakkan or Kumar. In the northwest, near the border with Turkey, the village of Sheklab and its 100 inhabitants were buried.
January 26, 1967	Chicago, Illinois, northwest portions of the state of Indiana, and into the southwestern parts of lower Michigan.	Considered the "worst blizzard" in the history of a city widely known for harsh winter weather. Known as the "Blizzard of 1967," the storm struck an area from southwest lower Michigan, through northwest portions of Indiana, and in to the city itself. Chicago saw a record amount of snow for a 24-hour period-23 inches (58 centimeters).
March1993	Regions of Southern Canada, the New England, Mid-South, and Southeastern U.S., Cuba, and areas in and around the Gulf of Mexico.	Known as the "Storm of the Century" and/or the "1993 Superstorm," this late winter storm unleashed a series of storm-related events (tornadoes, severe thunderstorms, windstorms, and blizzards) across an area encompassing more land at one time than any other storm in recorded history.
March 11-14, 1888	Sections of the U.S. East Coast (including areas of the states of New Jersey, New York, Massachusetts, and Connecticut,).	Also known as the "Great White Hurricane," this storm is considered by some weather historians the worst blizzard in American history. Areas of New England were paralyzed with snowfall totals of between 20–60 in. (51–150 cm), and wind speeds of more than 45

		mph (72 km/h). There were cases of snowdrifts left behind in the wake of the storm that towered more than 50 ft. (15 m). Railroads were shut down and people were confined to their houses for up to a week

Glossary of Blizzard/Winter-Related Terms

Blizzard- A type of extreme winter storm characterized by winds of at least 35 mph (56 km/h), reduced visibility of less than 1/4th of a mile (less than 400 meters), and very cold temperatures for at least 3 consecutive hours. In most blizzards, the wind gusts typically exceed the 35 mph/56 km/h, while visibility can be less than 1/4th of a mile—both for more than the 3 hours minimum criteria.

Blizzard Warning- is a weather advisory is issued by the National Weather Service when blizzard conditions are imminent within 12 to 24 hours from the time the warning is issued. These conditions include the presence of winds of at least 35 mph (56 km/h), falling and/or blowing snow, reduced visibility of 1/4th of a mile (0.4 km) or less, and low temperature—all for 3 hours or more. These are the most dangerous winter storms, and can be especially severe when combined with temperatures below 10 degrees.

Blizzard Watch- is a weather advisory issued by the National Weather Service when the possibility of conditions related to a blizzard are expected between 12 and 48 hours from the time the watch is issued. These conditions include the presence of winds of at least 35 mph (56 km/h), falling and/or blowing snow, reduced visibility of 1/4th of a mile (0.4 km) or less, and low temperature—all for 3 hours or more.

Freezing Rain/Freezing Drizzle- is a type of precipitation that occurs when super-cooled rain or drizzle freezes upon contact with surfaces such as the ground, trees, power lines, etc.

Frostbite- is a medical conditions resulting in the damage to skin tissues, caused by prolonged exposure to cold temperatures. Untreated severe frostbite can lead to injury and/or destruction of skin and underlying tissues—most often that of the nose, ears, fingers, or toes—which may lead to the necessity to amputate dead skin.

Ground Blizzard- is defined as loose snow or ice that is blown by strong winds embedded in the vicinity of a storm. Though not true blizzards in the meteorological sense, ground blizzards occur when snow from a previous winter storm or snow even is blown through the air, creating conditions similar to those found in actual blizzards. As such, ground blizzards do not result in the accumulation of more snow totals.

Hypothermia- is a medical emergency that occurs when the human body loses heat faster than it is able to produce it, causing the body's core temperature to fall to dangerously low levels. Whereas the normal core temperature of the human body is around 98.6 F (37 C), the body temperatures of individuals suffering from hypothermia drops to 95 F (35 C) or below. When the body's temperature drops to this point, the functions of the heart, nervous system, and other vital organs begins to become impeded. Left untreated, hypothermia can eventually lead to complete heart failure and respiratory failure...and eventually death.

Lake-Effect Blizzard- is the blizzard-like conditions resulting from lake-effect snow. Under certain conditions, strong winds can accompany lake-effect snows creating blizzard-like conditions. The general difference between actual blizzards and lake-effect blizzards is the duration of the events; lake-effect blizzards tend to last less than the 3 hour threshold required for recognition of an actual blizzard.

Lake-Effect Snow- is a weather-related phenomenon that occurs when a mass of sufficiently cold air moves over a body of warmer water (such as a large lake). The result is the buildup of clouds over the water/lake. The variances in temperatures causes show showers to develop as the clouds move downwind of the body of water. The intensity of lake effect snow is increased when higher elevations downwind of the lake force the cold, snow-producing air to rise even further.

Lake-Effect Snow Belts- is a term describing of a number of regions in and around the Great Lakes in North America where heavy snowfall in the form of lake-effect snow is particularly common. "Snowbelts" are typically found downwind of the lakes, principally off the eastern and southern shores.

Whiteout- is a weather-related condition caused by intense gusts of winds, usually associated with the winter season. In a whiteout, visibility is rapidly reduced to the point where sight of the immediate surroundings is severely hindered by blowing snow.

Wind-Chill (Factor)- is the combination of wind speed and the air temperature, as it affects exposed human skin. As the wind blows faster and the temperature drops, more of the body's heat is lost more rapidly—making a person feel colder even though the air temperature remains the same.

Appendix A:

Winter storm watches, warnings, and advisories are issued by local National Weather Service Forecast offices.

Winter Weather Outlook - is a statement issued when there is a chance of a major winter storms from 3 to 5 days in the future. This is meant to assist people with their long range plans. The advanced nature of these particular forecast statements tends to limit its general accuracy overall.

Winter Storm Watch – is a statement indicating the possibility of hazardous winter weather that may include the presence of. Winter storm watches are issued at least 12 hours, but usually no more than 48 hours before the hazardous winter weather is expected to begin.

Winter Storm Warning – is issued when a winter storm that may include heavy snow, sleet, or ice accumulation from freezing rain is imminent, or has a high probability of occurring within 36 hours. A Winter storm warning is issued when the possibility of between 4 inches (10 cm) to 7 inches (18 cm) will likely fall in the warning area (in the Southern United States, where severe winter weather is much less common and any snow is a more significant event, warning criteria are lower, as low as 2 inches or 5.1 cm).

Freezing Rain Advisory - is an advisory issued when freezing rain (or freezing drizzle) is expected to cause significant inconveniences, but does not meet warning criteria (typically greater than 1/4 inch or 6.4 mm of ice accumulation).

Ice Storm Warning – is issued when heavy accumulation of ice due to freezing rain will likely cause downed trees and power lines. Electricity and/or other services may be disrupted for an extended period of time (in extreme cases). Traffic arteries may become impassable for most vehicles.

Blizzard Warning - is a weather warning issued when conditions indicate the possibility of strong winds (at least 35 mph or 56 km/h), very low visibility (less than 14th of a mile or .40 meters) due to blowing or falling snow, and cold temperatures (i.e., wind chills).

Wind Chill Warning - means that conditions, based on a combination of wind and air temperatures, are imminent. This means that conditions will deteriorate to the point where life-threatening wind chill temperatures of -40 F/-40C (or less) for at least 3 hours. Exposure to this combination of strong winds and low temperatures without protective clothing can quickly lead to frostbite and/or hypothermia. Longer exposures can be fatal.

Winter Weather Advisory (For Snow) - is issued for snowfall between 4 and 7 inches (10 and 17 cm) within a 24 hour period.

Blowing Snow Advisory - This is issued when visibility is expected to be reduced due to blowing snow and increased winds.

Wind Chill Advisory - means that conditions, based on a combination of wind and air temperatures, are imminent. This means that conditions will deteriorate to the point where life-threatening wind chill temperatures of -25 F/-31C (or less) for at least 3 hours. Exposure to this combination of strong winds and low temperatures without protective clothing can quickly lead to frostbite and/or hypothermia.

The No-Nonsense Guide To Blizzard Safety

Lake-Effect Snow Watch - is issued when there is a possibility of heavy lake effect snow of accumulations totaling 7 inches (17 cm) or more within a 12 hour period).   A lake-effect snow watch is issued at least 12 hours before the snow is expected to begin

Lake-Effect Snow Warning -is a type weather advisory issued when heavy lake effect snow is either imminent, occurring, or has a very high probability of occurring within the next 12 hours. Expected snow totals under a lake-effect snow warning are usually expected to be at least 7 inches (17 cm), and may be accompanied by strong winds.

Lake-Effect Snow Advisory - is an advisory generally issued for areas in and around the Great Lakes (also around the Great Salt Lake in Utah) when snowfall accumulations are expected to total between 4 and 7 (10 and 18 cm) inches within a 12-hour period.

Frost/Freeze Warning – is issued whenever the possibility of below-freezing temperatures is likely, which may cause significant damage to plants, crops, or fruit trees.

Appendix B
Federal Emergency Management Agency (FEMA) contact information by region

As an extensive government agency, FEMA administrative resources (as well as contact information) have been somewhat decentralized. This is to say that, in order to expedite any assistance to local and state governments (and to limit the potential for bureaucratic confusion), FEMA was divided into regional offices that oversee regional "zones." These *Regional Operations Offices* serve as the arms of the central agency's headquarters (located in Washington D.C.) and through which all policy, managerial, resource and administrative actions effecting coordination between headquarters are initiated.

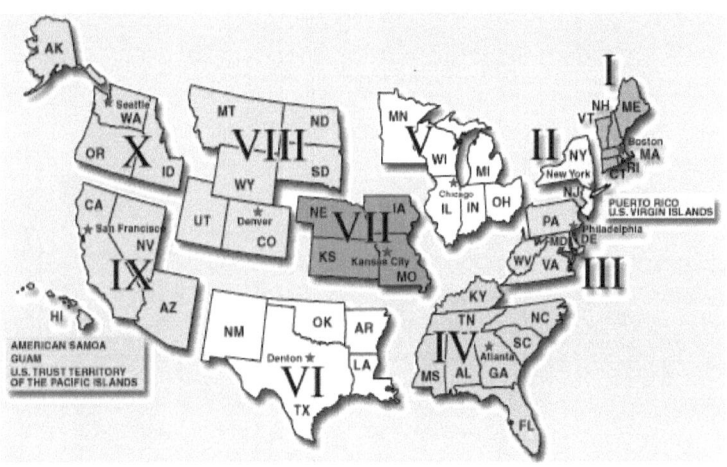

Region	Location	States Serving
Region I	Boston, MA	CT, MA, ME, NH, RI, VT
Region II	New York, NY	NJ, NY, PR, USVI
Region III	Philadelphia, PA	DC, DE, MD, PA, VA, WV
Region IV	Atlanta, GA	AL, FL, GA, KY, MS, NC, SC, TN
Region V	Chicago, IL	IL, IN, MI, MN, OH, WI
Region VI	Denton, TX	AR, LA, NM, OK, TX

The No-Nonsense Guide To Blizzard Safety

Region	Location	States Serving
Region VII	Kansas City, MO	IA, KS, MO, NE
Region VIII	Denver, CO	CO, MT, ND, SD, UT, WY
Region IX	Oakland, CA	AZ, CA, HI, NV, GU, AS, CNMI, RMI, FM
Region X	Bothell, WA	AK, ID, OR, WA

Contact:

FEMA Region I
99 High St.
Boston, MA 02110
1-877-336-2734
Email

Federal Region II
26 Federal Plaza
New York, NY 10278-0002
Telephone: (212) 680-3600
FEMA-R2-ExternalAffairs@fema.dhs.gov

Puerto Rico and Virgin Islands

Mailing address:
Carribean Division
PO Box 70105
San Juan PR 00936-0105

Physical address:
New San Juan Office Bldg
159 Calle Chardon, 6th Floor
Hato Rey, PR 00918
Telephone: (787) 296-3500

FEMA Region III
One Independence Mall, 6th Floor
615 Chestnut Street
Philadelphia, PA 19106-4404
(215) 931-5500

FEMA Region IV
Federal Emergency Management Agency
3003 Chamblee Tucker Road
Atlanta, GA 30341

Office: 770-220-5200
Fax Number: 770-220-5230

FEMA Region V
Federal Emergency Management Agency
536 South Clark Street, 6th Floor
Chicago, IL 60605
(312) 408-5500

FEMA Region VI
Federal Emergency Management Agency
FRC 800 North Loop 288
Denton, TX 76209-3698
E-Mail: FEMA-R6-RRCC-PrivateSector@fema.dhs.gov
Tribal Affairs
E-Mail Norma.Reyes@fema.dhs.gov
Telephone: 940-898-5233

FEMA Region VII or Federal Emergency Management Agency
9221 Ward Parkway, Suite 300
Kansas City, MO. 64114-3372
Telephone: (816) 283-7061
Tribal Contact
E-mail: jonathan.weinberg@fema.dhs.gov
Telephone: (816) 809-4128

FEMA Region VIII or Federal Emergency Management Agency
Federal Emergency Management Agency
Denver Federal Center
Building 710, Box 25267
Denver, CO 80225-0267
(303) 235-4800

FEMA Region IX
1111 Broadway, Oakland, CA 94607
Phone:(510) 627-7140
Pacific Area Office
(808) 851-7900
Southern California Field Office
(626) 431-3000

FEMA Region X or Federal Emergency Management Agency
Federal Regional Center
130 - 228th Street, Southwest
Bothell, WA 98021-8627
(425) 487-4600

Appendix C:

Similar to the opposite form of skin damage—burns—frostbite has varying degrees of severity. This is to say that the longer the exposure to the cold, the more extensive the potential damage to skin tissue that results.

First degree

The first or initial level of frostbite is known as "frostnip." Frostnip affects the surface layer of skin that has been exposed to the cold. When this level of frostbite sets in, there is usually a level of itching and pain—after which, the skin develops white, red, and yellow patches and becomes numb. This level of frostbite usually does not result in any level of permanent skin damaged, as only the skin's top layers are affected. However, in some cases long-term insensitivity to both heat and cold can sometimes occur after suffering from frost nip.

Second degree

If exposure to the cold continues, second degree frostbite begins to set in. At this level, the skin tends to freeze and harden. However, the deep skin tissues are not affected as yet (deeper skin tissue will usually remain soft and retain its normal levels of elasticity and functions). In cases of second-degree frostbite, blisters will begin to form 1–2 days after becoming frozen. The blisters may become hardened and appear black in color. Fortunately, the injuries incurred at this level of frostbite tend to heal in about a month. Still, the affected areas may become permanently insensitive to both heat and cold.

Third and fourth degrees

When the effects of long-term exposure to cold temperatures continue uninterrupted—or when the initial phases of frostbite are not addressed medically—deep frostbite occurs. At this dangerous stage of frostbite, the muscles, tendons, blood vessels, and nerves all freeze. The skin will be hardened, accompanied by a waxy feels. The loss of temperature sensitivity becomes more extreme, and in some cases permanent. The appearance of the area of skin affected by third-degree frostbite will usually be covered with purple-colored blisters at first, which eventually turn black and become filled with blood. If the affected are(s) becomes infected with gangrene, this extreme form of frostbite may need to be amputated; if left untreated, these parts of the body may fall off, especially in the case of fingers and toes. It may take up to several months to accurately assess the extent of damage done to affected areas of skin as attempts are made to help (or wait until) the damaged skin heals on its own. During this time, affected skin tissue could be dead or dying, and causing the potential for more damage.

Appendix D:
How to drive in hazardous winter/blizzard-related conditions

Driving

1.   When it comes to blizzards and other severe winter storms, the best course of action is simply to avoid driving in such hazardous—if it can be avoided. But in the event that driving in such conditions becomes necessary (such as in emergencies), it is best to at least wait until snow plows and sanding/salting trucks have had a chance to operate on snow-covered roads.
2.   Leave early and allow for extra time to reach destinations. This prevents the likelihood that speeding—and an increased risk for accidents—will occur.
3.   Vehicles which are likely to be used in driving in the winter should be winterized (i.e., prepared properly) in order to function at optimum levels during the harsher winter conditions.
4.   If unfamiliar with driving in snowy conditions, consider practicing winter driving techniques in a snowy, open parking lot in order to familiarize one 'self with how a vehicle handles and reacts in such conditions
5.   When driving on icy and slick roads, driving speed should be decreased, and distance between vehicles should be increased in order to provide plenty of stopping space (a good rule of thumb is to place about 3 times the normal space between an operating vehicle and the nearest vehicle in front).
6.   Apply brakes gently to avoid skidding. In the event that wheels lock up, let up on the break,
7.   Lights should be turned on to increase visibility to other motorists. Also, lights and windshields should remain clean and clear of snow at all times.
8.   The use of lower gears provides tractions, especially on hills.
9.   Avoid using cruise control or overdrive on icy roads.
10. Extra caution should be applied to driving on bridges, overpasses and infrequently traveled roads. These surfaces tend to freeze first, making them especially hazardous. Even at temperatures above freezing, ice may form in shady areas or on exposed roadways like bridges.
11. The urge to pass slower-driving snow plows and sanding trucks should be avoided for the simple reason that the road in front of plows tends to have more hazardous driving conditions than the road behind the plows.

12. Avoid over-confidence. All types of vehicles are vulnerable to potential trouble on icy roads, so the assumption that a particular vehicle can handle most conditions should be avoided. Even four-wheel and front-wheel drive vehicles can encounter trouble on winter roads.

Skids/Skidding

1. If a vehicle starts to skid, the foot should be taken off the accelerator/gas paddle.
2. Skidding vehicles should be steered in the direction in which the vehicle is sliding and/ or skidding; if the vehicle's wheels are sliding left, then the vehicle should be steered to the left also. The same holds true if the vehicle is skidding towards the right.
3. If the vehicle is skidding from the rear (i.e., the rear tires are skidding as opposed to the front), steer the vehicle in the direction the wheels are skidding/sliding. If during this attempt to correct the slide the vehicle begins to slide/skid in the opposite direction, then the wheels should also be steered in the changed direction to regain control of the vehicle. It might actually be necessary to steer a vehicle several times left and right in this manner before regaining complete control of the vehicle.
4. For vehicles with standard breaks, brakes should be pumped gently during this correction maneuver to regain control. Vehicles equipped with anti-lock brakes (ABS) should have steady pressure applied to the brakes (there will be a pulsing feel from the brakes if this is done correctly). Avoid the inclination to pump the brakes.
5. If a vehicle is skidding due to the front wheels, the foot should be immediately taken off the accelerator and the vehicle shifted in neutral. Avoid immediately steering corrections.
6. As the vehicle begins to skid sideways, the now-sideways facing wheels will begin slowing the vehicle—causing traction to be regained. As this occurs, the vehicle should then be easier to steer in the direction the driver wants the vehicle to go. As steering is slowly returned under control, the transmission should be placed in "drive" and the vehicle gently accelerated.

Entrenched/trapped vehicles

1. Avoid the urge to accelerate the vehicle in place (i.e., do not spin the vehicle's wheels). Doing so will only cause the vehicle to dig deeper in the spot in which it is stuck.
2. The vehicle's wheels should be turned/steered side-to-side several times in order to push snow out of the way.
3. A light touch should be applied (on the accelerator) in order to ease the vehicle out of the spot.
4. A shovel or other digging instrument should be used to clear snow away from the wheels and underside of the vehicle.
5. Sand, kitty litter, gravel, or salt should be poured in the path of the wheels in order to gain traction. After this, the vehicle should be "rocked" back and forth (shifting the transmission from "forward" to "reverse" while attempting to drive the vehicle loose from where it is stuck.[22] Shift from forward to reverse, and back again. Each time the vehicle is in gear, a light touch should be applied to the accelerator until the vehicle starts to move.

---

[22] Please consult a vehicle's owner's manual before attempting to "rock" a vehicle loose from being impacted by snow by constantly shifting the gears. Doing so can damage the transmission on some vehicle models.

The No-Nonsense Guide To Blizzard Safety

Appendix E:
Useful Smart Phones & Computer App (Applications)

1. <u>Weather Bug</u> (Free)

An all-around weather app for both phones and computers (<u>Weather Bug Desktop</u>), Weather Bug provides real-time weather forecasts for the users' vicinity for a 10-day period. In addition, this app contains a real-time sensor that warns of dangerous lightning threats for the users' area. Created and sponsored by Earth Networks.

2. <u>The Weather Channel</u> (Free)

Also available for <u>desktop/laptop</u> computers , this app—like Weather Bug—provides an active 10-day weather forecast for the user vicinity. In addition, the issues real-time severe weather bulletins such as those issued for blizzards.

Many other similar applications of various costs can be found by searching various online application sources such as <u>Google Play</u> and the Apple-supported <u>i-Tunes</u> .

Index

The No-Nonsense Guide To Blizzard Safety

References

"Blizzards." Secrets of the Earth. The Weather Channel. Aired: July 4 2013. Time-Warner Cable

"Blizzard Unexpectedly hits North Dakota and Minnesota." Retrieved 21 July, 2013 from The History Channel website.

Buckley, B., Hopkins, E., & Whitaker, R. (2004). "Weather, a Visual Guide." Sydney, NSW, Australia. Firefly Books.

"Carbon Monoxide Poisoning." Retrieved July 21, 2012, from the Centers for Disease Control website.

Cummings, James. "What to do about frozen pipes." Chicago Tribune. 9 Jan 2004. Print.

Davey, Monica & Fitzsimmons. E. G. "Chicago Humbled by Powerful Storm." New York Times. 2 Feb 2011 Print.

Ford, Alyssa. "125 Years Ago, Deadly 'Children's Blizzard' Blasted Minnesota." (11 January 2013). Retrieved 20 Jul 2013 from the Minnesota Post website.

"Hundred injured as blizzard causes Canada car pile-ups." (22 March 2013). Associated Press Retrieved 6 June 2013 from The National.ae website.

"Hypothermia," Mayo Clinic Staff. Retrieved July 19 2013 from The Mayo Clinic website.

Mogil, Michael. H. (2007). "Extreme Weather: Understanding the Science of Hurricanes, Tornadoes, Floods, Heat Waves, Snow Storms, Global Warming and Other Atmospheric Disturbances." New York, NY. Black Dog & Leventhal Publishers, Inc.

Ostro, Stu. "Blizzards." Retrieved 22 July 2013 from The Weather Channel Website.

The No-Nonsense Guide To Blizzard Safety

Pearson. Michael. "Blizzard Blasts Upper Midwest." Retrieved 2 August 2013 from Cable News Network (CNN) website.

Skilling, Tom. "Ask Tom Why: What is the Difference between a Blizzard And a Ground Blizzard, And a Winter Storm And a Snowstorm?" Chicago Tribune 11 Dec 2011. Print.

Taylor, Charles (ed.) (2011). "The Kingfisher Science Encyclopedia." London, UK. Kingfisher & MacMillan Children's Books.

"Wet vs. Powdery Snow." (12 November 2013) Retrieved 20 Nov 2013) from AccuWeather.com website.

"Warm Water and Cold Air: The Science Behind Lake-Effect Snow" Retrieved 1 August 2013 from the website of the National Oceanic and Atmospheric Administration (NOAA).

"What To Do if Stranded in Vehicle During a Blizzard." Retrieved 23 July 2012 from the city of Denver, Colorado Office of Emergency management website.

"What To Do If Trapped In Your Car During A Blizzard." Retrieved 23 July 2013 from KCBD television website.

"Why Talk About Winter Storms?" Retrieved 24 July 2013 from the Disaster Center website.

"Winter Storms & Extreme Cold." Retrieved 24 July 2013 from Ready.Gov website

"Winter Storms: During the Storm." (12 December 2012) Retrieved 23 July 2013 from The Weather Channel Website.

"Winter Storm Preparedness ." Retrieved 26 July 2013 from the American Red Cross website.

Zhorov, Irina. "Why Did South Dakota Snowstorm Kill So Many Cattle?" (22 October 13). Retrieved 23 Oct 2013 from National Geographic website.

Picture Credits

Cover
KOTA TV website
http://mytown.kotatv.com/wyoming/2013/10/03/gillette-declares-snow-emergency-2/

"March 9-10 Blizzard in North Dakota." High Plains Regional Climate Center website
http://www.hprcc.unl.edu/articles/index.php?id=76

Wikipedia Images

Andy Manis/Getty Images, "Blizzard Paralyzes Much of Midwest." New York Times, 9 Dec 2009.

ABC News Website

"John F. Kennedy (JFK) Airport Flight Delays: Blizzard Expected to Cause Flight Delays in New York, Boston.
"WILA TV website.

Page 3
Chicago Tribune Online
http://www.chicagotribune.com/news/photo/chi-110203-snow-aerials-blizzard-2011-pictures,0,1368459.photogallery

Page 4
http://boston.cbslocal.com/photo-galleries/2011/01/12/january-blizzard-the-damage/http://www.aliraqi.org/forums/showthread.php?t=97514&page=2

Page 6

The No-Nonsense Guide To Blizzard Safety

http://library.thinkquest.org/C0126189/blizzard_formation.htm

Page 7
"March 9-10 Blizzard in North Dakota." High Plains Regional Climate Center website
http://www.hprcc.unl.edu/articles/index.php?id=76

Page 12
CBS Boston.com

Page 14
http://www.weather.com/outlook/weather-news/news/articles/blizzard-march-midwest_2011-03-03?page=2

Page 16
Wikipedia Images

Page 25
"Emergency snow shelters."
http://www.examiner.com/article/emergency-snow-shelters

The No-Nonsense Guide To Blizzard Safety

Other Books in the No-Nonsense Safety Guide Series

Published By Lulu Books & Beyond The Spectrum

The No-Nonsense Guide To Tornado Safety

• Paperback: 84 pages • Publisher: lulu.com (November 22, 2013) • Language: English • ISBN-10: 1304648648 • ISBN-13: 978-1304648648 • Product Dimensions: 9 x 6 x 0.2 inches • Shipping Weight: 6.4 ounce

The No-Nonsense Guide To Blizzard Safety

The No-Nonsense Guide To Blizzard Safety

• Paperback: 54 pages • Publisher: lulu.com (December 21, 2013) • Language: English • ISBN-10: 9781304709394 •
Product Dimensions: 9 x 6 x 0.2 inches • Shipping Weight: 0.28 pounds

The No-Nonsense Guide To Flood Safety.

• Paperback: 60 pages • Publisher: lulu.com (November 22, 2013) • Language: English • ISBN-10: 1304648613 •
Product Dimensions: 9 x 6 x 0.2 inches

The No-Nonsense Guide To Hurricane Safety.

• Paperback: 59 pages • Publisher: lulu.com (December 20, 2013) • Language: English • ISBN-10: 9781304733030 •
Product Dimensions: 9 x 6 x 0.2 inches

Other upcoming books in the series include: "The No-Nonsense Guide to Fire Safety," The No-Nonsense Guide To
Earthquake Safety," and "The No-Nonsense Guide To Automobile Safety."

www.ingramcontent.com/pod-product-compliance
Lightning Source LLC
Chambersburg PA
CBHW050341290526
45785CB00006B/2587